Hey Beautiful Girl! Book of Affirmations for Girls

I AM and God Reaffirms Me!

ISBN: 978-1-7350143-3-3

I0142961

Publisher and Editor: Fiery Beacon Publishing House, LLC

Fiery Beacon Consulting and Publishing Group

This work was produced in Greensboro, North Carolina, United States of America.

Hey Beautiful Girl!

Book of Affirmations for Girls

I AM and God Reaffirms Me

By

Madelyn G. Jones

Table of Contents

Acknowledgements

First, I want to thank God for giving me the thought to even write my first book. God you awe me!

I would like to thank my husband Jared, and my three beautiful children Malachi, Madisyn, and Jared Maxton for selflessly permitting time and space for me to fulfill what once was only a dream. I love you all with every fiber of my being.

I want to thank my parents Pastor Ogden T. Jones and Sheryl Williams for their prayers, push, and love.

I would like to honor my spiritual leaders, Pastor Antoine and Shelley Carter Burton for their love support and prayers.

In addition, I want to honor Pastor Derrick and Roshonda Hawkins for their continuous support whether I am near or far.

Lastly, I would like to honor my coach Pastor Cassandra Elliott for stretching me beyond what I saw in front of me. I am forever grateful.

The Foreword

This book is for all my beautiful girls that have ever experienced trying to find themselves and where they fit in. When one struggles to discover their identity, they can become anxious, and at times overwhelmed. This book is to help our young girls, tweens, and teens so that we can break the mold of what the world and social media outlets are trying to convince them to be.

Many of our young ladies are battling peer pressure, issues with self-confidence, and some even stress as they are daily faced with challenges. This book will affirm them, but we know that the word of God will and can provide them with security and the peace that they long for.

The scriptures in the following chapters are uplifting and bring reassurance on your worth and value in the sight of our father, Jesus Christ. Our God has made each of you beautiful, strong, wonderful, and his has great purpose for your life.

You are Royalty

Royalty is a noun defined as:

"people of royal blood or status."

Beautiful girl since you are Royalty, and therefore, must act like it. Royalty is a mindset. When you know you are Royalty, you must think it and then it will manifest. When you are Royalty you operate in grace, class, and style. Royalty means that you understand that you are a daughter a king.

- **You have been born again into a royal family**
- **You have been given royal authority**

- **You have been given royal duties**

Knowing what our Father says about you and walking in His truth are two separate things.

Beautiful girl, I affirm you that "You are Royalty!" I reaffirm you by the word of God.

But you are chosen, race, a royal priesthood, a holy nation, a people for his own possession, that you may proclaim the excellencies of him who called you out of darkness into his marvelous light.

1 Peter 2:9

You shall be a crown of beauty in the hand of the

Lord, and a royal diadem in the hand of your

God.

Isaiah 62:3

But let your adorning be the hidden person of

the heart with the imperishable beauty of a

gentle and quiet spirit, which in God's sight is

very precious.

1 Peter 3:4

Do not let your adorning be external the braiding

of the hair and putting on of gold jewelry, or the

clothing you wear.

1 Peter 3:3

She makes bed coverings for herself; her clothing

is fine linen and purple.

Proverbs 31:22

Beautiful girl, the scriptures above are to always remind you that you are royalty. In the past three chapters of affirmations I pray that you now know with full understanding and without any doubt that you are loved, not alone, and royalty. May you never question in these areas again, and may you always see yourself through the lenses of our Father Jesus Christ.

Beautiful girl, you are amazing; never allow what society or social media platforms to predict your identity. Always find yourself remembering that you identify yourself with attributes of Christ. I leave with you thirty affirmations to recite one daily.

You are Loved

Loved is defined as:

a verb (used with object) to have love or

affection for, to have profoundly tender,

passionate affection for (another person), to

have a strong liking for.

Beautiful girl, God loves us. We sometimes know

it in our minds, but oftentimes, we do not live a

life that says that we are confident in His love for

us. Here are a few things that God's love does for

us:

- God's love comforts us

- God's love is poured into us through the Holy Spirit

- God's love is unchanging and steadfast

- God's love convicts us

- God's love heals us

- God's love compels us to love one another

- God's love compels us to love ourselves

- God reveals his love to us through Jesus Christ

Beautiful girl, I affirm you that "You are Loved!"

I reaffirm you by the word of God...

Deuteronomy 7:9

Know therefore that the Lord your God is God, the

faithful God who keeps covenant and steadfast

love with those who love him and keep his

commandments, to a thousand generations.

Psalms 86:15

But you, O Lord are a God merciful and gracious,

slow to anger and abounding in steadfast love and

faithfulness.

Psalm 136:26

Give thanks to the God of heaven, for his

steadfast love endures forever.

John 3:16

For God so loved the world, that he gave his only

Son, that whoever believes in him should not

perish but have eternal life.

Beautiful girls, allow these scriptures to build

your confidence in knowing that you are loved.

You are Never Alone

Alone can be defined as:

an adjective, "having no one present," or as an adverb, "as on one's own. "

Beautiful girls, many times in our minds we believe it when God says are never alone, but there are times in our lives when circumstances cause us to question if he is present. Here are a few things to remind us that God never leaves us alone:

God is with us always.

God is always protecting us.

God is always waiting to hear from us.

God makes time for us.

God intercedes for us.

Beautiful girl, I affirm you that "You are never alone." I reaffirm you by the word of God.

Deuteronomy 31:8

It is the Lord who goes before you. He will be with you; he will not leave you nor forsake you. Do not fear or be dismayed.

Deuteronomy 4:31

For the Lord your God is a merciful God. He will not leave you or destroy you or forget the covenant with your fathers that he swore to them.

Matthew 28:20

...And behold, I am with you always, to the end of the age.

Psalm 27:10

For my father and mother have forsaken me, but the Lord will take me in.

Beautiful girls allow these scriptures to always remind you, that you are never alone.

30 -Day Affirmations

Day 1

I am authentically and unapologetically me.

Day 2

I speak success over my life, and it will manifest.

Day 3

I am the Daughter of the King!

Day 4

I have no regrets - only tools to help me better
accomplish my goals.

Day 5

I am my own biggest fan!

Day 6

I choose to be happy, so today will be full of happiness.

Day 7

I am not afraid to ask for help. I am fearless.

Day 8

I am proud to represent the values of my family as well as myself.

Day 9

My dreams are obtainable.

Day 10

My voice and opinion matter.

Day 11

Others are cruel and that reflects who they are, I do not have to be cruel in return.

Day 12

I am responsible with the things that matter to me.

Day 13

I will not live in the shadows of others. I will create my own way.

Day 14

I can say "no" and mean it.

Day 15

I will love myself unconditionally.

Day 16

I will embrace my flaws, and not self-sabotage.

Day 17

I will excel in my academics.

Day 18

I will make God and my parents proud.

Day 19

I will be okay with being set apart; I will not try to fit in.

Day 20

I am not lost - I am still in creating mode of myself.

Day 21

Difficult times may arise, but I will not stop going.

Day 22

I cannot even fathom all that I am capable of.

Day 23

I will enjoy my youth.

Day 24

I will be trustworthy and loyal to myself and others.

Day 25

I will walk in grace and extend grace to others.

Day 26

I am enough.

Day 27

I am the very handiwork of my Father's (Jesus) hands.

Day 28

I will begin each day with an affirmation and leave each day with gratitude.

Day 29

I have all that I need to be successful.

Day 30

I am becoming the best version of myself. My journey begins today and ends with me fulfilling and living out my purpose.

May these affirmations help you navigate through your days. Yes, you are perfect just the way you are. Do not change for others, and always remember to show up for yourselves. This book was written with you in mind, and daily you navigate through the many challenges of life. You are beautiful, strong, courageous, honorable, valuable, loved, appreciated, needed, and created just the way God intended.

Connect with the Author

Madelyn G. Jones

Wife| Mother| Mentor|
Entrepreneur |
Owner/Visionary of
Behind Her Eyes
Mentoring, LLC

Madelyn G. Jones is a

native and resident of

Baltimore, Maryland. For

seven years, from 2010 until 2017, the Lord shifted

her to Greensboro, North Carolina. During that

season of her life, the Lord allowed her to find her

healing that she so longed for. Madelyn was

licensed as a minister to preach the gospel on June

23, 2014, in Thomasville, NC at then, Word Empowerment Christian Center. She relocated back home to Maryland in June of 2017. She currently serves in ministry as an armor bearer to her Pastor, Pastor Shelley Carter Burton of Changing Lives Ministries of Baltimore, and as an intercessor, and exhorter. Under her current Pastors/Spiritual Parents Pastor Antoine and Shelley Carter Burton, Madelyn has been stretched and challenged to go all the way in God.

Since that time, Madelyn married in October 2014, her husband Jared Jones, and has partnered with him to walk fully in her purpose and calling. Madelyn began the vision of Behind Her Eyes Mentoring in 2015. During this time, she knew that God had called her to minister and mentor to younger women. During her prayer time with God, He showed her the purpose in the many things she had to experience and how it was going to be used to bless and enhance the lives of others. While in North Carolina, Madelyn did not feel the timing was right, so she took a back seat on the vision, while pursuing the more of God on a deeper and more intimate level. Under the leadership of her former Pastor Derrick Hawkins and Lady Roshonda Hawkins at The Refuge Greensboro, she was in training to become an ordained Deacon in the Lord's church; she was taught discipleship and had to undergo much training.

In the marketplace, Madelyn currently has sixteen years in Healthcare and Healthcare

Management. She looks to obtain a Bachelor of Science degree in Business Management in the Spring of 2021. Madelyn launched and rebirthed Behind Her Eyes Mentoring, LLC in April 2020 right amidst a global pandemic. Madelyn has seen the hand of the Lord move upon this vision because she submitted herself to God and rendered a "Yes" that she stands solid on. The launching and birthing of this vision has caused God to smile and breathe upon it. Madelyn's heart and passion is to see young girls, "tweens," and teens become healed, whole, and empowered. Her favorite scripture to share is Psalms139:14 NIV: **"I praise you because I am fearfully and wonderfully made; your works are wonderful, I know that full well."**

Madelyn is the daughter of Pastor Ogden T. Jones and Deacon Sheryl Breeden Williams. They were her first teachers of the word of God and intercession. Madelyn is the blessed wife of Jared Jones and proud mother of Malachi, Madisyn, and Jared Maxton. She has one brother Marcus (Kenneith, wife) Jones. Madelyn believes in having a strong family foundation and prides herself on her first ministry which is at home. Madelyn loves God, is a worshipper, and loves to bless God in praise. Madelyn sings, and for many years, taught liturgical dance. Madelyn's hobbies include reading, writing, singing, and dancing. Madelyn is eternally grateful to God that he continues to download in her the vision with clarity and revelation. Madelyn always says no matter what she is doing "I just want to make Daddy (Jesus) proud!" That is the most important thing to her, not titles, nor fame, but knowing that God is pleased with her.

Facebook:

https://www.facebook.com/**BehindHerEyesMentoringLLC**

Instagram:

https://instagram.com/bhementoring2020

Spreaker Radio:

https://www.spreaker.com/user/12199061

www.ingramcontent.com/pod-product-compliance
Lightning Source LLC
LaVergne TN
LVHW021549080426
835509LV00019B/2921